WORDS FOR A LOST YEAR

MURRAY SHUGARS

POEMS

Linocuts by

CHAD POOVEY

DOS MADRES

2023

DOS MADRES PRESS INC.
P.O. Box 294, Loveland, Ohio 45140
www.dosmadres.com   editor@dosmadres.com

Dos Madres is dedicated to the belief that the small press is essential to the vitality of contemporary literature as a carrier of the new voice, as well as the older, sometimes forgotten voices of the past. And in an ever more virtual world, to the creation of fine books pleasing to the eye and hand.

Dos Madres is named in honor of Vera Murphy and Libbie Hughes, the "Dos Madres" whose contributions have made this press possible.

Dos Madres Press, Inc. is an Ohio Not For Profit Corporation and a 501 (c) (3) qualified public charity. Contributions are tax deductible.

Executive Editor: Robert J. Murphy

Illustration & Book Design: Elizabeth H. Murphy
www.illusionstudios.net

Typeset in Adobe Garamond Pro & Bell MT
ISBN 978-1-953252-97-5
Library of Congress Control Number: 2023949086

First Edition
Copyright 2023 Murray Shugars
Published by Dos Madres Press, Inc.

ACKNOWLEDGEMENTS

"Cedar Cigar Box," "Fin-de-Siècle America," and "Caught Up in Absolute Gravitation" first appeared in *The Café Review* (Winter 2019).

Thank you to my daughter Miranda Shugars and to my friends Daniel Todd and Chad Poovey for offering gracious feedback on drafts of this manuscript.

LINOCUTS BY CHAD POOVEY

COVER: Empty Mailboxes
Page 1: Sunrise
Page 5: Live Oak
Page 23: Cypress
Page 41: Pines
Page 55: Crows
Page 71: Moon View of Earth
Page 78: Author portrait
Page 79: Artist portrait

For Sandy

TABLE OF CONTENTS

The Trouble with Trying to Know
    Someone Somewhere 1

SPRING
The Words That Come Between Us 7
Filling the Empty Quiver of Spring 9
These Failures of Spring 10
When the Levees Broke and the Moon
    Surrendered the Stars 11
Wild Strawberries 12
What the Crow Showed Me 13
No Further Than Forgotten 14
In Your Arms 16
Where You Find Me 17
Where I Find You 18
When the Geese Return 19
When You Come to Vicksburg 20

SUMMER
Tangled in Wrinkled Air 25
My Shadow Over the Immediate 27
A World Where We Are Possible 28
Tonight the Stitches in My Lips like
    Angry Whiskers 30
Cedar Cigar Box 31

How We Talk to Us 32

To Know Your Little Secret 33

Problems That Turn into Rain at Night 34

Closer to the Gods That Made Us 36

When Our Dancing's Done 37

Beneath a Sun that Blood Offers 38

Night Comes Quick. 39

FALL

Throats in a Tumult and Devouring Discourse 43

Evening in the Coppered Hills 44

Fin-de-Siècle America. 45

What We Tell Ourselves 46

Caught Up in Absolute Gravitation 47

The Drowned Man. 48

When I Come to You. 49

When You Found an Uncanny Lostness 50

Wind-Kindled Gaze. 51

Raindrops on the Windowpane 52

Between the Act and The Matter of Fact. 53

Dried Flowers. 54

WINTER

And We Suffer a Most Untheatrical Life. 57

News and Morning Music 58

Prayer for the Living. 59

If You Guess My Three Names 60

What It Means to You 61

Lonely for Your Benignity 62

Day of Wind-Broken Birds. 63

As If We Could Live Forever in a Lightning Flash 64

Just Enough Light to Live in the Eye 65

The Friendly Neighbors 66

Time Doesn't Pass We Do 67

Last Words for a Lost Year 68

POSTSCRIPT

The Problem with Trying to Measure
    What I Feel for You 73

About the Author. 78

About the Artist 79

WORDS FOR A LOST YEAR

The Trouble with Trying to Know Someone Somewhere

> The *thing-in-itself* (which would be, precisely, pure truth,
> truth without consequences) is impossible even for the
> creator of language to grasp, and indeed this is not at all
> desirable.
>> —Friedrich Nietzsche, "On Truth and Lying in a
>> Non-Moral Sense"

> Pain always produces logic, which is very bad for you.
>> —Frank O'Hara, "Personism: A Manifesto"

Here I am on a southern sidewalk
Standing at a lamppost and holding an umbrella
Thinking about the words of Frank O'Hara
And you again

Distant as drizzle over the Pacific
Near as night mist rising from the Mississippi
Fog pooling in low fields and lapping at the hills

I remember you
Wore a cotton dress and leather sandals
Your toenails painted with the Stars and Stripes

You were laughing and laughing
Blue eyes white teeth red lips
A face the colors of America

I remember your carless hand
Resting on my shoulder
Your eyes when you said—
If you have to fight a war that's over nothing
Then you better join the side that's gonna win

I am writing a poem
Not about a flag
Nor about a song about a flag

I am writing a poem about the year's first flowers
Blooming in strange domains of language

O lovely stranger

I'm writing a poem
About us

* * *

I remember the hard-parched hills
The chaparral slopes and pine peaks
Of your nettled landscape

I remember the light of your metropolis
Was a little bored and disgusted
Light lost in the alleys of your yellow city
Light longing to be near us

Now I'm back in Vicksburg
Where night's wet grass
Glistens grayly under streetlamps
Here where fortuity blesses our difference
Here where to be
Not what one seems
But quixotically becomes

Here where heal-all and prairie phlox bloomed
On Independence Day 1863
When Pemberton surrendered his sword to Grant
Flowers that gave the lie to a fallen city
And gave the lie to ironic guns and the sorry rig of refugees
That gave the lie to twenty-thousand killed and wounded
    soldiers

* * *

Maybe your English teacher
Warned against getting bluer
Against going on and on
Like nightfulness like the dark

She believed in the rules of poetry
An elaborate symmetrical order
Like the big porticos and inflated columns
Of Warren County's antebellum courthouse
Where riverboat tourists pose for family photos

But where
During the massacre of 1874
Reconstruction finally failed in Vicksburg Mississippi
When a White mob stormed the building
Ousting Black elected leaders
And lynching dozens of Black citizens
And where
In years to come
White leaders wielded Jim Crow justice

Many decades passed before the town
Officially celebrated the Fourth of July

You live in a place with no memory of an enemy's boot
Is that why ennui stains your city's light?

* * *

I remember the cadence of your steps up a blind staircase
Ending at a door that might have opened on the void
Maybe you were reading too much
French poetry

Words you still feel but can't remember
And may never see again
Like phantom limbs

We have dreamt a space inside us
Dark and small enough for infinite silence

You're so beautiful
Who would ever dare to love you?

SPRING

The Words That Come Between Us

I'd like to start where clouds
Unravel common prose

A drizzly evening in Mississippi
When we sit beneath the dripping eaves

It could be my birthday
And you could tell my cards

An ear attuned to that elusive ambiguity
As meaning flees your fingertips
Along a trembling thread of language

O sweet
Disorder of your rococo hair
As you lean close to say—
I don't know if they have much
Faith in us as all that

Not a single moth
Attacks the porch light

You give me the river

You give me both
Lanes of that country blacktop
One coming and one going

You say—
Does it hurt
Is all I meant to say

Come sunup
The brush we piled to burn
Begins to bud

Filling the Empty Quiver of Spring

Tonight my thoughts
Forge the silent dance of one
Dark arrow then another

Tonight the impassable river rises
And the catfish war begins

Look!
Garcia Lorca's rooster moon
Crows in the air above your shoulder

O how slate gray clouds
With a blind archer's breathless aim
Arrive all the way from Spain

Tonight my soul sets off
Down fresh-tilled cotton rows
Whistling a song skinned like a catfish

And you with a thousand
Voices on your shoulders
Arouse a gnawing wind
And spectacular arrowheads of rain

These Failures of Spring

What am I to do with the rising river
This hole in my head
And National Poetry Month?

It's all like when I first
Discovered sex and soda pop
Not in that order

I was like
O sweet angels in heaven what
My parents never told me!

Back then
I knew this girl who carved
Rumors of love around the schoolyard

When the Levees Broke
and the Moon Surrendered the Stars

Each morning she watched me
Make chalk drawings on the blackboard
Before other students
Shuffled in to first hour English

I drew the cloud cats
Dancing with the rain fish
I drew the blue 'coon
And the haunted playground
I drew the doomed river's
Dime-store soliloquy
The wounded moon's final phase
I drew the buzz saw at Wilson's Mill
Screaming through pine logs
I drew the sawdust piling up
Faster than the shadow boy could sweep

She folded the note
She left on my desk
Into a paper crane

Wild Strawberries

Let's collide like a pair of horses
Galloping in spring's last meadow

Let's go to all our favorite places

The countryside of lost gardens
The dirt road of lucky bloodshed
The levee of feathers you sleep on
The canebrake of my spent speed
The ravine of unraveled laughter
The river of youth and shame
The ditch of the red-winged blackbird

Wild strawberries will eat our shadows

What the Crow Showed Me

I had no use for words
No use to feel
The triple wind
The tripped and fickle
Words I couldn't say

A thirsty bird
I swallowed loss
Drank coffee in a demitasse
And saw my mother's cotton sheet
Douse dawn and dream the wrinkled day

And I broke my wings on songs
My father couldn't play

No Further Than Forgotten

When as if entangled in dry air
A memory opens like a dark rose
And you lean close again to whisper—

Your breath caressing my neck
Your curls touching my cheek—
I can't sleep

Night unbuttons my mind

I think of your lips
Your mouth a pink rosette
O sweet cockade of passion!

Several festivals inside me
Await your voice
At the opening ceremonies

My heart's a cavernous ballroom
Where we could dance among the mirrors

I have chasms of air inside me—
Hear my dry yawp
Echo in your city's yellow canyons

Until I saw you
I never knew a woman
Without a shadow

O fire of naked flowers

Since I came home
Spring squats on bare haunches
The hungry season waits
Like a dog in the road

In Your Arms

—for Johanna (& Patch, born 28 March 2022)

The evening stone's cool belly knows you
And midnight's dry shade
Knows you knows your breath your lips
Your voice and the lullaby you sing
To the infant boy you hold in your arms

Tomorrow comes with small white fingers
Closing in a fist around your thumb
As the distant highway yawns awake
And the hills open one eye to watch
You holding a child in your arms

The wind and the fig tree know you
The little ponies in the field across the road
Know you and the flies in your own house
They know you and the child of sunlight
You hold in your arms

In your arms in your arms
How you hold in your arms
The source of a river
The thin cry of a lost moment
Waiting ten thousand years
For this boy's eyes to open

Where You Find Me

Not the rhythmic pulse of stars
But the lulls between the beats
Make you want to dance

Swing with stellar lacunae
Sway with ellipses that trace
The mute cadence of the cosmos

Not history's thump and flutter
But dusty sun-shafts piercing this room
Move you to sing

Song of the tongue's fist
Song that seeps behind the eyes
Song of the winged stigmata
Song of the bird
Wounded by the wind

Not the snarl of the swelling river
But foam at the flood crest
Unlocks a language

Decipher the cuneiform characters
Of the moon's crucifixion

Translate my eyes
Gazing at these root-sighing trees

The curls of your hair
Breathe like Spanish moss

Where I Find You

I saw you in Vicksburg
Dancing in the dusky dissonance
So above it all
Like wind-kissed wisteria
Or a little smoke

You were never where you stood

I saw you in Muskegon
When the blossoms whirled
In their approximate silence
New but hardly novel
The old hours arranged
According to whatever
Lipstick you wore

You were never where you stood

I saw you in Poughkeepsie
Tasting a discarded flake of sky
And telling midnight how to dream
Biblical calamities

I saw you in Los Angeles
When you said here is a hand
And here is another and yes
I believed it I wanted to believe

When the Geese Return

I imagine you somewhere
North of here

Winter's final flakes
Or maybe pear blossoms
Drifting in the corners of your garden

Cowbirds gather on your lawn
Trilling liquidly to one another
A language you half-remember

You stand at a river crossing
Where the deep shoal
Owns your heart

Willow branches drag in the current

Hidden in the clouds
Wild geese call

When You Come to Vicksburg

Will you take a boat?

The possibilities for visions grow
The closer you get
You also might like to know
Vicksburg's lousy with quizzicalness too

That's okay
My door's open to spring rain on the magnolia

You could put out your hand—
The purest fragments the clearest
Residue of mislaid sound

You could say dawn
Sometimes revives a curious plant
Which might symbolize possibility
Or half a dozen other -ilities

And then again sometimes dawn
Undoes a sleeping dog
Vicksburg's lousy with undone hounds

Waking guests at antebellum B&Bs
Where you could take a selfie
With Yankee cannonballs lodged in parlor walls
Or dig up Minie balls buried in the flowerbeds

It wouldn't surprise me

If you had a vision when you get here
People have them quite a bit in Mississippi

Remember that afternoon on the escalator
When you said—
Going up for a change
Is all we really want

Now I'm only slightly piqued to find
My only slightly sullied wings
Hidden in your garretless eyes

Vicksburg's lonely without
Your irreprovably sour smile

How many teeth
Have chewed this
Piece of eternity?

My solitude has your face
Your sigh-colored hair
Your silence that comes as a kiss

What I really want to say is
When will your boat
Arrive at the landing?

SUMMER

Tangled in Wrinkled Air

I'm trying
I'm trying to sleep
But I keep hearing you say—
Love's wherever I see dogs
Peanuts and pigeons
Some hilltop city park
Where everyone's happy for a change

Think of all the things
Reflected in the dark
Lenses of your borrowed sunglasses
All those eye-strain days
All the summers too bright
When breathing was impossible

April's gone so's May now June
Lurches pensively across Mississippi
Searching for a color Miró might've used
Your eyes a color Miró drew

I'm getting tired of not dreaming
Summer afternoons in a painting by Bruegel
Instead of scenes from The Last
Judgment of Hieronymus Bosch

I remember the nearness of our faces
There on that garden bench
Your mischievous eyes your lips
Your rapid but pleasantly minty words

Remember how we said
Night's white asterisks
Would form any goddamn constellation
We drew with a blade of wildrye?

Ecstasies—what a funny word—came near
When the moon opened
Our hands

God we were fine for a minute or two!

Now I can't look in my eyes
Without seeing yours

I've had enough of boutique mirrors
Framed in pebble and driftwood
They're so frank I don't care
How old the house they hang in is

Tonight I want to be alone
Which is why
The river reminds me of nothing

Out there beyond my window
I hear the solitude of trees
Rubbing trees

They're not really alone are they?

My Shadow Over the Immediate

Wake up!

Put on your magenta pout
Your paisley skirt your daisy
Go-go boots the color of desire

Night ends!

Lemons and oranges grow in your yard—
O paradise—they await your eyes
In the city's yawning orchards

Translate dawn's tattooed songs
Interpret chords of toppled shadows

Conceive O daughter of a rugged land
How can you conceive such terra-cotta music?

Amid the vertical suburbs
Solitude listens for you
A timelier silence you can't imagine

Throw off the sheets and open the window
Hear the birds hunting for clarity—
A gift you receive so quietly

As I lean close
Nearly kiss you just to see
The faint veins of your eyelids
Breathing bluely in this morning's light

A World Where We Are Possible

Is this first light
The light we're looking for?

The sun shines upside down and sings
This morning under stones
And dawn bleeds up a rocky slope

So what?

So what if we say
It might be nice to go away
Together

So what if we
Fall into the final lunacy

So we're taking off
Our shadows are we?

We're putting on our shiny grins

After all
We are English majors

We know all the words
But not their feelings

We are poetic today but we are not
Too poetic we are not poetic at all

We know when we are good
Even if no one else knows

We know when we are bad
We're better

Hot damn!

Let's dance our hidden rhythms
Let's dream our furtive verses

Let's wake
In a world where we are possible

Tonight the Stitches in My Lips
like Angry Whiskers

Teach me the language of shadows
Words furtive as foxes
Prowling a Mississippi neighborhood
The smell of burnt umber
As if all the streetlights cast the same aroma
In fine pools one-two-three-four and so on
Down the otherwise dark avenue

Where a fox
Slouches from yard to yard
Pausing only to pounce
Beneath first this then that magnolia looking for
What? maybe something even God won't lay
Prometheus-like into my open palms—
A desire that heaven knows
Goes down the sinuous water
Rushing in the empty blood of wisteria

Cedar Cigar Box

I can put any memory you like
In here—

Maybe something I read in a history book
A dry galantine served to obese monks
Doomed for the guillotine three days hence

The proud head of a galloping pony
I saw at a county fair when I was twelve

The gallant lungs of a mudfish breathing
Hoarsely—anything I can remember
However big or small will fit here

The sound of a loud laugh suddenly
Broken by a lover's frown
A horse's whinny or panther's purr
The shape of a fist or violin

The carnivorous eye of a panting sparrow
I saw in the desert near Mosul
During a combat patrol

Everything that passes
Through the forehead of a lonesome buzzard

Every dancing every danceable decision
I wish I'd made before the lid fell

How We Talk to Us

We hear only ash announced in silence
These words we stir like powdery silt
A dry skoosh that withers in our bodies
These arid syllables that name our sand

This murmur burns its ancient incense
The muttering odor of an old wound
The brittle fragrance of panting soot
The mumbling hard-parched smell of dust

We give each other windswept aromas
These desiccated consonants and vowels
Quietly stale and only slightly sun-bleached
Loaves we break and eat and call our love

To Know Your Little Secret

I might change
The color of my thoughts for you
Dancing in the smoke-blue light of memory

You who spent my quarters
Swaying at a jukebox in that dress
Just to show how music teaches us to lose

Another life
Than the one we're living now
Or to live the one we're losing

And I see exactly what you mean
I see the stoic lesson
You learned from Alexander Pope

That whatever is
Is right

I see a rose a rose a rose
Of dawn ungiving night
My breath tasting of a Gertrude Stein cigar

I'd share such mouthless moments
I'd sooth words from sunscald water
I'd ride shank's mare a hundred miles
Just to know your little secret

Problems That Turn into Rain at Night

No it was a cheap picnic
Like taking a short sip of a thick book
For instance reading in *Moby Dick*
Only the chapter on the whiteness of the whale
And even then skipping whole paragraphs
Just to say you got through it

Yes I unzipped the flowers
Only minutes before you arrived
So you'd see their open hearts
Beating shyly through Persian blinds
As you hesitated at the window
Deciding whether to knock

No I believe vistas out this window
Are parts of speech tangled
Not in the memory of a lost map
But in horizons of two-bit proverbs
Misplaced in the dim light
Falling into darkness into quiet water

Yes I really don't know that I want
To talk about that anymore after all
It's likely raining somewhere
That Paul Éluard and I once tossed
Love's dice while arguing the delicate
Problem of the firefly and that bastard
Won the game so I slouched off to write
Innumerable sonnets I never sent you

No the skin all dressed up as you say
Is a sort of abomination maybe so
But what about the simple apple
Fluent in the secret language of color
Whose skin flames minty French green
Duck egg blue chartreuse avocado
Goldenrod sunflower dried blood
Mahogany amber saffron yellow bird shit?

Yes I suppose the tuning fork vibrates
Indefinitely when a thirsty soul cuts
Time in half like a ruby grapefruit
Thick pink juice dripping throatward
Which whenever I see it always makes me
Feel like a small fictional nincompoop

No my dear I dance
In a shower of warm music
On the dubious roof I built to play
Four open notes on a resonant mouth harp
And you're here too my love your body
A shimmer in the air beside me
As we enter my stigmatized attic
Throwing off the rain impatiently

Yes we run away perilously with our life
Wearing each other's clothes as we kiss
Our open palms goodbye one at a time
All thirty-five of them the way the dead
Play piano without hands without sound

Closer to the Gods That Made Us

We're exactly at the urgent orchards when
The moon resounds like a knock on a door
And we refuse O we refuse to say
Moonstruck though the word is on these
Voluptuous pears we can smell the sound
Sexy and simple as fear the way dim light
Falters beneath these trees the way
We hear a crisp guitar and faint castanets
And as we dance a three-time jig a bruised fog
Floods the hysterical grove a sluggish knee-deep
Current pushing our legs with languid boredom
The way the devil's clerks recite fiercely slow
Inventories of what and in what language?

When Our Dancing's Done

Let's be startled by sexy marginalia in an old Bible
Let's take off our meaningful glances one foot
At a time like stockings labeled as artful hints and
Why don't we dangle them out the window
Draping those mildly frowning socks over
The nearest branch—you know the tree I mean
The oak which you said has no impossibilities
The oak under which I said how can we fail
The momentary smile of down-dappled sunlight?
And remember when I said it how you named me
Gerrymander Hoppy-Shins and I called you
Irrepressible Joy That Fits and then we looked up
And saw the shimmering wings of a cerulean sky
The air becoming air before our eyes

Beneath a Sun That Blood Offers

You've lived long enough
In the desert of a stranger's mind

You walk through an art nouveau gate
And enter a garden of seven wells

A lavender meadow
Where mossy pines dream
The silk cheek of a valley

An off-kilter sky of lavishly carved clouds—
Smoke thick from the heart

And the barrens of a stranger's face
His mouth a singed O a scorched
Hole in the air between you
Exhaling an odor of stifled words

Maybe you will pour
Your voice down his desiccated throat

Maybe you'll invent a lipstick
Like a French poem that chokes roses

Night Comes Quick

Here you are in Vicksburg
City of gray twilight and drowsy windows

Hiding out at the hostelry
Sitting on a cast iron bench at the courthouse museum
Ignoring a sandwich and tea under the live oak

Dreadful and jocund journeys brought you here
Where the prince of lies waits and ages

You sometimes dream of swallowing your hands

You watch the wretched tourist families
They believe in God no doubt they pray
They feed the pigeons what pigeons
More like sparrows and these people
Their smell fills the air like faith in a lonesome star

You know all
Even the lonely ones have
Or will have one day betrayed their lovers
One way or another

The seams of their lives go to your heart

You think of an eiderdown pillow

Tonight you will dream of milking
Snake venom into heirloom teacups

A child is singing a song about a broken promise
A song of love and infidelity

You are alone a bell cries day's end
I told you night draws up fast this time of year

In the gloom two gray shapes are receding

FALL

Throats in a Tumult and Devouring Discourse

Time being no necessary adjunct or true
Ornament of love we invent
Barbarous recipes for ancient syllables
Hunted in a father's thicket
Snared in a mother's thistle

We wait on a porch for noon
Sipping tumblers of lukewarm lies
Gnawing the dry bone of hope

For once in our life forget that we live
Like Adam and Eve
Forget that we forgot that we
Never left this fallow and fallen garden

Beneath the bridge of our arms
Flows the choked bayou of our conversation

All we want is to explore illimitable desire
The strange domain of silence of no
Words a mute wilderness where we
Finally find and kill the noble beast

In a savage land
There are no vegetarians

Evening in the Coppered Hills

Your fear of not being
Makes you intimate with stones

And your fear of missing
The slow movement of shadows—
Their quiet breathing
Their whispers—
Makes you kin to silence

Insects pause at your hunting boots
Nothing's out of season

Fin-de-Siècle America

Carriages were passing in the distance
When I took my first drink of your dantesque
Dreams and of course I ate a tawdry thought
Or two O remember how we emptied
Every drop of pleasure from the vessel
Long before the mountains were burning
Before we were dying of loneliness
Back when fog parted down the middle
Of any road we walked where you told me
Good God what's there to be common about?

Lift the tureen's lid and ladle me out
A steaming mug of your sweet somber soul

Let's drink this burning liquor like your life
Your sun-severed and windblown life

What We Tell Ourselves

O darling!
What good does it do
To say death dwells in the hearts of poets?

Smiling arrows pierce our sides

Don't we laugh when we lose
The frozen beads of our eyes?

Soul grief's a chuckle
We hear every convulsive night
And one or two dyslexic days

We tell ourselves
This comforting story—

A hanged god adores a cosmic rope
And the rope adores a solar wind

And the wind
If it ever settles down
Enjoys the harlequin burlesques we dream

When dawn fails to laugh and can't quite
Love or hate us as much as we'd like

Caught Up in Absolute Gravitation

It's true
Antonin Artaud told us

Life consists of burning up questions
Sharp sensations in our limbs
Stilettos of ice lodged in our throats

A naked foot
Ripples the black water of our love
A shivering pane of star-swerved sound
Immoderate ecstasy or anger
The whole goddamn Milky Way
Hurling over us

Night's blurred voice
Scrapes against the earth
A low mutter over cold stones
A thin untethered scuff—a moonlit scrap
Tangled in the toils of desire
Igniting constellations in our eyes

The Drowned Man

Look! do you see these words
Inside me loosely turning
These enormous
Flies I call blood

Do you see these unzipped jeans
I call American persuasion

As I lie here
Tiresomely shirtless at the swollen
River so dangerously supple this time of year

So svelte-muscled
That three coal barges
Hit the bridge and they go down

Have your eyes always been too blue for autumn

Have your hands always been as careless
As oak leaves exiled on the current

Look! do you see this gray light
Lull the sky

Do you see the drowned man
Seek the earth
Set in your clay pot

When I Come to You

I come walking
Desire's arduous path

I who
Like water going to the grassy edge
Have no power to affect anything
That matters

I who come
With my losses intact and find
Everything already here
At the end of a fitful sky
Where one makes do with a future
In which great things might happen

I with my tail in my mouth
And my mouth in a song
About your singular smile
Which no one loves
More than I

I on whom daylight—
Leaning its weight homeward
Over the Mississippi River—
Settles with valley clarity
As thin as a song
Full of treason and ruinous wind

When You Found an Uncanny Lostness

Once
You heard mindwings flutter
Down they came
Untangled for a change

Flushed thought
Shook windowbranches

Metaphorstorm

Pricked by the slightest wordspur
Winsome-hoofed shadows
Whinnied and galloped

All whisper-maned and moon-striven
All mute-kissed by the blind mouth

Once
You found yourself
Unseen but felt
Eye-stung by the hornet-star

Word-grasping in slivered light
Word-gasping in sickled night

Wind-Kindled Gaze

And then one day you wake
Crows into untouchable leagues of desert sky

Your eyes inspire dawn so bluely
Waking day's nocturnal wings

O daughter of solitude
See how morning answers you
How dayflame flowers in the window

See beyond the patio
Fallen oranges flaming in the dirt

You have waited all your life
For desire's dry wind to ignite
The hidden syllables of your name

You have waited for me
To tell about the secret stones
I picked up in this blazing desert

Come sit at the breakfast table
So you can eat my burning eyes

Raindrops on the Windowpane

She follows lost water in the falling evening
She whispers
But I keep forgetting what she says

She walks the halls of horoscopes
Kissing cards of silence

She crinkles her face
When she laughs at the bottom of the stairs

She offers her remote presence
Her sweet-strange air
Those moments from another life

When she smiles
She spreads the lips of simultaneity

She hangs her tapestry in my head

She puts on a shroud and clenches
Night's reigns in her teeth

Her body opens and her voice glows

She strokes the ribs of my last dream
Dancing in her quiet rooms

Between the Act and The Matter of Fact

When I imagine your wanton whispers
My threadbare tympanum trembles thinly

These days I feel like a t-shirt
Hanging grayly from a doorknob

These days
All the words I fling at the universe
Can't escape their eccentric orbits
And boomerang back upon me
Here in the dry outskirts of profundity

You say that my poems lack
Thematic content of the kind
The word poetry in the full
Virtue of its meaning signifies

Far stars evaporate

Even this mug of tepid tea
Has a faint taint of complaisance

You say poets
Who never use a past participle
Deserve the eternity they strive for

Dried Flowers

There's a different person in each
Sparkling occasion and yes
A polished mirror likely frowns
When I touch the lip of your glass

But who cares
It's night we're together and we hear
Ocean currents maybe darkness
Move in the drowned cockpits of a lost squadron

Though I don't know
From whale bate really
Because our words dart off
Like shimmering minnows believe me
I think of you in that city all your life
A necklace of jewel-like moments this one too!

I think of a photo you took of dried flowers
You might have meant to water

WINTER

And We Suffer a Most Untheatrical Life

Rain thrums the roof and rat-a-tats the window
Just as the winter voices you imagine in the Bible
And in Goethe where even the ink has its own
Thoughts of paradise and you can forget about
Italian beaches and the pleasure of being
Together in the same darkish garden watching
The same moonish paving stone sink into a path
That might have led toward terrible terrible youth
The heart empty in its knowledge of unaquaintance
The way you walk in your best outfit alone at night
Loveless and lampless down the same lane where
One hot Mississippi afternoon we saw the river
Flow past Vicksburg looking as tepid and tan
As the milk and coffee in our daughter's cup

News and Morning Music

We scared up just enough money to chase
Life into our arms
Winter flowers pretending to sleep

We did more than play
At the game of existence

We touched interplanetary distances
Caressed a nebula's trembling nervous system
Felt amazed by great suffering
Snared by these indifferent stars

Startled by our love
The moon mistook us
For a pair of stones beneath the waves

The ocean offered us
Those pebbles of sound
We kept in our pockets

We came back to the house
Calm and warm
My muse a pal who passed
For you with news and morning music

Prayer for the Living

Despite all these dead
We leave behind waiting for us
Eventually to join them like snow
Floating flake by flake
Up into the sky's open mouth

Despite leagues of snow
That separate us
We care nothing for grief
Or the bitter season of cold
On this fine long journey
Through steps of unfinished nights

That end with us hearing
All those ecstatic
Noises inside us

If You Guess My Three Names

One of me hunts
An angel's trumpet and a serpent's eyes
One of me bejewels every sun-struck snowflake
One of me whistles off the trigger finger

One of my naked selves
Searches out the desert snowstorm
One of my sleeping selves rises coolly skyward
Flaunting boredom's borders
One of my quietly sexy selves
Lodges in your actual mind
A vague desire prodding you
To write a beautiful poem

One of me waits for you
Like a warm day in December
One of me waits for you
Tonight at the Versailles
One of me waits for you
Tomorrow morning at 6:00 o'clock
Waking from a dream and saying
You are gorgeous and I'm coming

What It Means to You

For a moment and then
Briars at best bitterly
Exhort night for feathered laughter
And yesterday still under snow
Listens for daybreak to inscribe
Its cold passage
When trees itch with winter sparrows
That quicken the slowness of dawn

You think you know what it means
But not too soon at last
You know the impulsiveness of God
The beardless clear-eyed moon
Offering a subtle grin and the first
Dark speech of morning

Lonely for Your Benignity

To be as free and witty as you
Whose rococo hair refuses angels' combs
And all unchanging things

Well that's okay
After all
There's no snow in Hollywood
Where fame crosses its knees and spits
Thin light one fears along the walks
And shaded ways
As in parting when something
Flutters between us

We never understand
That feathered light

And it's then you say
I'm supernatural
After all there's the steady
Wind of the spirit to consider and yes
Eventually death

Mountains tremble blah blah blah
Constellations whimper O panic
Of a closed rose intentionally alluring

Zounds!

I'm sober nonetheless and lonely
For your benignity

Don't mention my fears to the fellas won't you

Day of Wind-Broken Birds

As if exactly the only way all this
Inexorably somehow moves us
Somehow tumbles us like torn leaves
Skittering into wet winter drifts—
O tree-eager night play windy chords
For us wear out your lousy instruments
You don't know you don't know what
Music should do for such lovers as we
Who palmed church pennies
We who wheedled from God's hand
Three sacred days alone together
We who care nothing for fragrant spring
A flagrant landscape gaudy with lust
A bawdy horizon fallen into itself and lost

As If We Could Live Forever
in a Lightning Flash

Cherishing those reflections you amble all
Sparrowy as if you don't give a good goddamn
Humming imperceptible sentiments as usual
Beneath great grieving towers of a desiccated city
O I know you love to read by candlelight I know
Drizzling rain a blind river and martyred trees I have
All these words and I ride like a dark horseman
Upon your soul-shade under wet leaves and
I imagine how you shut a window and douse
A light precise as an old engraving good
God let's just be here let's just ignore
Your seething city my river and be lost
Somewhere flowers get up especially early
When cars purr and foghorns moan and we do too

Just Enough Light to Live in the Eye

Then too when yesterday arrives
And I look especially shitty in the mirror
Shaving and mad at my performance
In last night's nightmare recently ended
Saying to my face why didn't you
Pocket those magic emeralds
You damned fool and I keep
Trying to remember something then
When afternoon later appears
Swaying loosely in the living room
Like an alcoholic Christmas tree
That's when I recall I dreamed you
Wielding the violent violin of desire
And playing the holy fuck out of it

The Friendly Neighbors

We thought we were the friendly neighbors
Waving at our grins across a backyard slope
We who breathed the catechism of frozen roses
The fragrant redemption of hidden thorns
The savage grass the desperate trees O why
Did we dimple when we glimpsed clandestine
Minarets and secret steeples impaling streets
Of mute desires and wordless tongues
Bleeding for the cataclysm of flowers and dry lips
Whispering wounded canticles and calls for prayer
The selves we had yet to meet we who felt just
Fine brooding over books now and then looking
Up to smile at our own smiles months went by
Years across the vast escarpment of our love

Time Doesn't Pass We Do

We miss us not because we love us
But because we've got no one else to hate

We know such incoherencies of life
If indeed we reach old age we know
Each leaf here beside a withered name

We whom stars love to dream
Let alone sleep
What shall we pray?

What word in what voice and in whose name
Shall we pray?

We do what we feel we do not even do
We do what we do not even know why we do

If we'd rather look at us
Than all those unpleasantly definitive
Portraits on museum walls
Then who's to say
We're cheated of some marvelous experience?

Last Words for a Lost Year

I dream of taking you again
To a shoreless alpine forest

I dream you one more
Evanescent sun-shorn song

A heavy but distant bell coughs and coughs
The final breath of a crucified year

Nothing delights you
More than churchy ceremonies

Your riotous curls
Tumble languorously over your face
And even if you open them
I won't see your opal eyes

See how I hide
Secret thoughts of you in snow
So I can dig them up

Nothing delights you more than churchy ceremonies

I etch your features in ice
Just to say my hand
Only my hand
Could have done this

I give you three
Feathers of agate darkness
I hacked up
Piecemeal from a wind-torn throat

I know that nothing delights you
More than churchy ceremonies

Which is why I give you this
Throat-raw song
Lost as a year's last words

POSTSCRIPT

The Problem with Trying to Measure
What I Feel for You

> Darkness was hidden by darkness in the beginning; with no distinguishing sign, all this was water. The life force that was covered with emptiness, that one arose through the power of heat.
>
> Desire came upon that one in the beginning; that was the first seed of mind. Poets seeking in their heart with wisdom found the bond of existence in non-existence.
>
> —"Creation Hymn," *The Rig Veda*, trans. by Wendy Doniger

> If the Eiffel Tower were now representing the world's age, the skin of paint on the pinnacle-knob at its summit would represent man's share of that age; and anybody would perceive that that skin was what the tower was built for. I reckon they would, I dunno.
>
> —Mark Twain, "Was the World Made for Man?"

My dear friend
Cosmologists tell our story this way—

That in the beginning
The universe was infinitesimally small
And many trillions of degrees hot

A singularity of unimaginable mass and heat
A subatomic point
Crushing everything into less than nothing
We could ever see

Richard Feynman in *Six Easy Pieces*
Illustrates atomic scale

By picturing an ordinary apple
Inflated as big as Earth

Each of its enlarged atoms
He says
Would now be the size of the original apple

And imagine within one apple-sized atom
A subatomic seed—
Still too small for naked eyes to see—
Enfolding all the congealed matter and energy of the cosmos

Think about it

Limitless primordial chaos
Aching to erupt—
As in so many creation myths

And this wee universe
Throbbing with cosmic ecstasy
Exploded and expanded at a staggering rate

Scientists assert
That for a fraction of a fraction of a second
In maybe ten to the negative thirty-something seconds
The universe grew faster than the speed of light
Driven apart by some form of antigravity

How to imagine
Such mind-boggling magnitudes?

Before inflation
The embryonic universe
Kicked against a quantum womb
Small and dark enough for infinite silence

In less than an instant
The infant universe inflated larger than a galaxy

And scientists tell us
The universe continues to expand
Beyond human observation
Its grand structures—its galaxies and clusters and superclusters—
Speeding away in all directions

They say
Distant light from most of the cosmos
Will never reach us

We can see only a fleck of everything

For a helpful analogy
Read Timothy Ferris's *The Whole Shebang*
Where he says
If the universe were the surface of Earth
Then what we could see of it
Would be smaller than a proton

Smaller than a proton

Think of the infinitely many
Events that unfolded

Since the Big Bang nearly fourteen billion years ago
And how those events had to unfold
Exactly as they did
To make a world
Where we are possible

Such thoughts humble and unnerve me
As when I reflect on the sublimity
I feel for you

About the Author

MURRAY SHUGARS, an English professor, lives with his wife, Sandra, in Vicksburg, Mississippi. He has published two previous poetry collections, *Songs My Mother Never Taught Me* (2010) and *Snakebit Kudzu* (2013), both with Dos Madres Press.

About the Artist

CHAD POOVEY is a sculptor and printmaker who occasionally writes fiction. His images in this volume are hand-printed linoleum cuts. His collection of short-stories, *Banana Taffy and Other Tales of Love, Madness, and Revenge*, was published in 2023.

OTHER BOOKS BY MURRAY SHUGARS
PUBLISHED BY DOS MADRES PRESS

SONGS MY MOTHER NEVER TAUGHT ME - 2009
SNAKEBIT KUDZU - 2013

FOR THE FULL DOS MADRES PRESS CATALOG:
www.dosmadres.com

www.ingramcontent.com/pod-product-compliance
Lightning Source LLC
Chambersburg PA
CBHW031448120626
46545CB00006B/2601